HILLARY IN GILO

Arthur J. Paone

HILLARY IN GILO

Copyright © 2007 by Arthur J. Paone

All rights reserved. Published by Belmar Publications
504 - 17th Avenue
Belmar, New Jersey 07719

Library of Congress Control Number: 2007905301
ISBN: 978-0-9746366-2-7

This is to acknowledge **Global Exchange** and the Bethlehem tour office of **Guiding Star** for helping me get around Palestine and meet some of its people.

Also by Belmar Publications:

Liberating Korea? (2003)   Arthur J. Paone
So Sue Me! (2004)   L. Meier and C. Cellini
(website: so-sue-me.com)

IN MEMORY

OF THE FOUR YOUNG GIRLS
WHOSE GOVERNMENT-SANCTIONED EXECUTIONS
BY ISRAELI SNIPERS
STARTED ME ON THIS QUEST.

Rawam Mohammed Abu Zaed, 3 years old
Islam Dwidar, 15
Tahreer Abu El Jidyani, 15
Iman Al-Hams, 13.

Each was killed with one or more
bullets to her head, in broad daylight,
to enforce a curfew or "security zone."

INTRODUCTION

Senator Hillary Clinton is not alone in seeking the approval of the Israeli Lobby. Every Presidential candidate has been walking down that well-worn path to swear allegiance to AIPAC (American Israel Public Affairs Committee).

Her pursuit, however, has been so shameless that it deserves special attention. It tells us much, if not everything, about the character of this person who wants to be our President.

Once viewed with suspicion by the pro-Israel Lobby because of her silence during a speech by Arafat's wife some years ago when Mrs. Clinton was First Lady, she has since worked her way into a position of almost absolute trust. Now AIPAC can count on her as "one of their own." Even before AIPAC sees a glint of anything appearing in Congress or a federal agency which might possibly be ambivalent about Israel or any of its myriad interests, Clinton pounces on it and chews it to pieces.

Israel wanted the US forcibly to change the government of Iraq. So Senator Clinton dutifully voted for that and has supported the war in Iraq for years.

Israel's number one foreign policy concern today has shifted to another neighbor, Iran. Almost every Jewish group in the world now has Iran at the top of its list of perceived threats to Israel. And again Senator Clinton runs along, this time trying to rush to the front of the Friends of Israel line by shouting alarms about Teheran's great menace to America itself. One could hear her now, as President, rattling sabers in the best Bush/Cheney fashion: ". . . all options are on the table."

On those days when Israel complains about Palestinian President Mahmoud Abbas as not being accommodating enough, Clinton reads him the riot act. On those days when Israel says nice things about a complaisant Abbas, she sends him flowers.

As part of constructing her super Pro-Israel persona, she went to Palestine in November of 2005. Standing on a rubble-strewed hilltop in an area which the Israelis call Gilo, she gave her blessings, with a smile, to the 30 foot concrete wall that was going up around Bethlehem. Like Bush uses the mantra, the "War on Terror," to justify his assault on the US Constitution, so Clinton repeatedly cited "Israel's Right to Defend Itself" to justify what former President Carter and most of the world considers an illegal structure that is doing grossly disproportionate harm to the Palestinians.

I have since visited this place called Gilo, in April and May of 2007. The Wall is now complete. It is a tragic scene. The "little town" of Bethlehem, the place of Christ's birth, has been cut off from its lifeblood communities, including Jerusalem, and is dying. The photos in this book, which I took, except for those otherwise noted, tell the surprising story of what I found in Gilo.

"[O]n this trip, I wanted to see the fence with my own eyes. . . . I stood on a hilltop in Gilo and received a detailed briefing from Col. Danny Tirza who oversees the Israeli government's strategy and construction of the security fence. . . ." (Quote and photo on right: Clinton website.)

"*Israelis have long had to make sacrifices in order to protect themselves. . . . In defeating terror, Israel's cause is our cause.*" (Quote: Clinton website. Photo: <u>Canadian Jewish News</u>, November 15, 2005.)

MAPS

JERUSALEM AND BETHLEHEM AREA

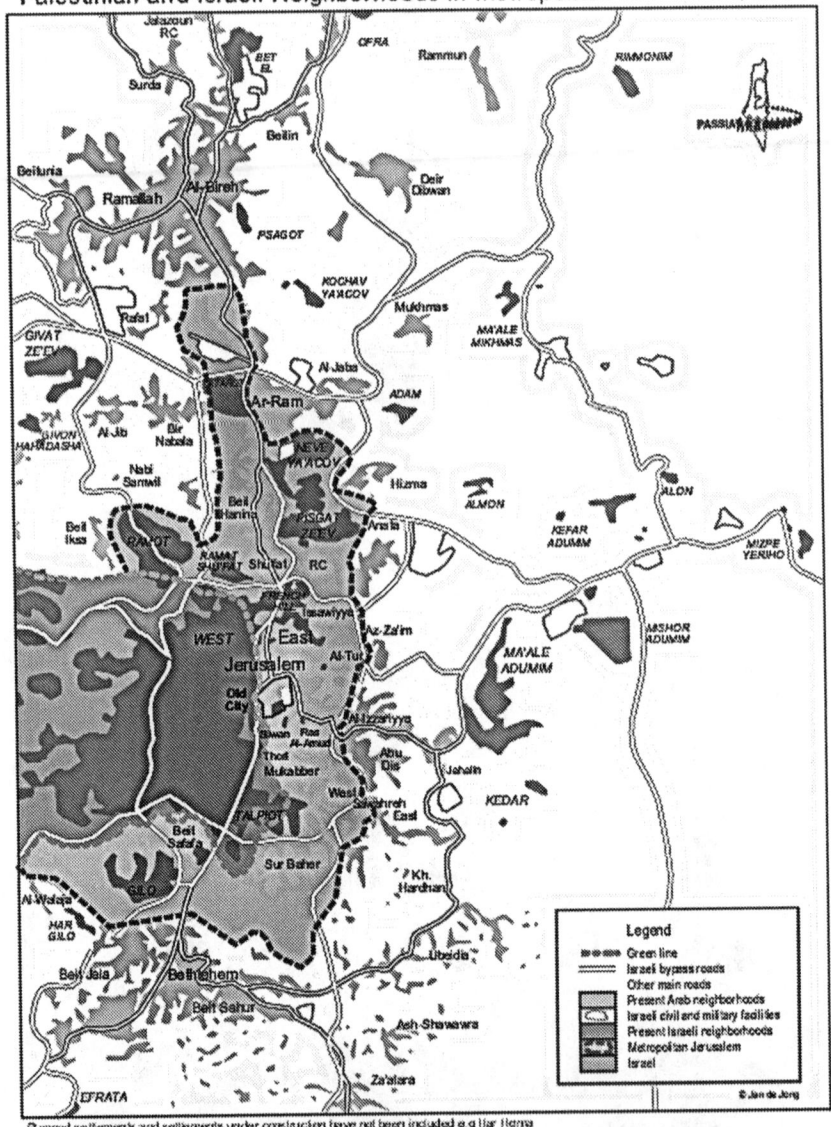

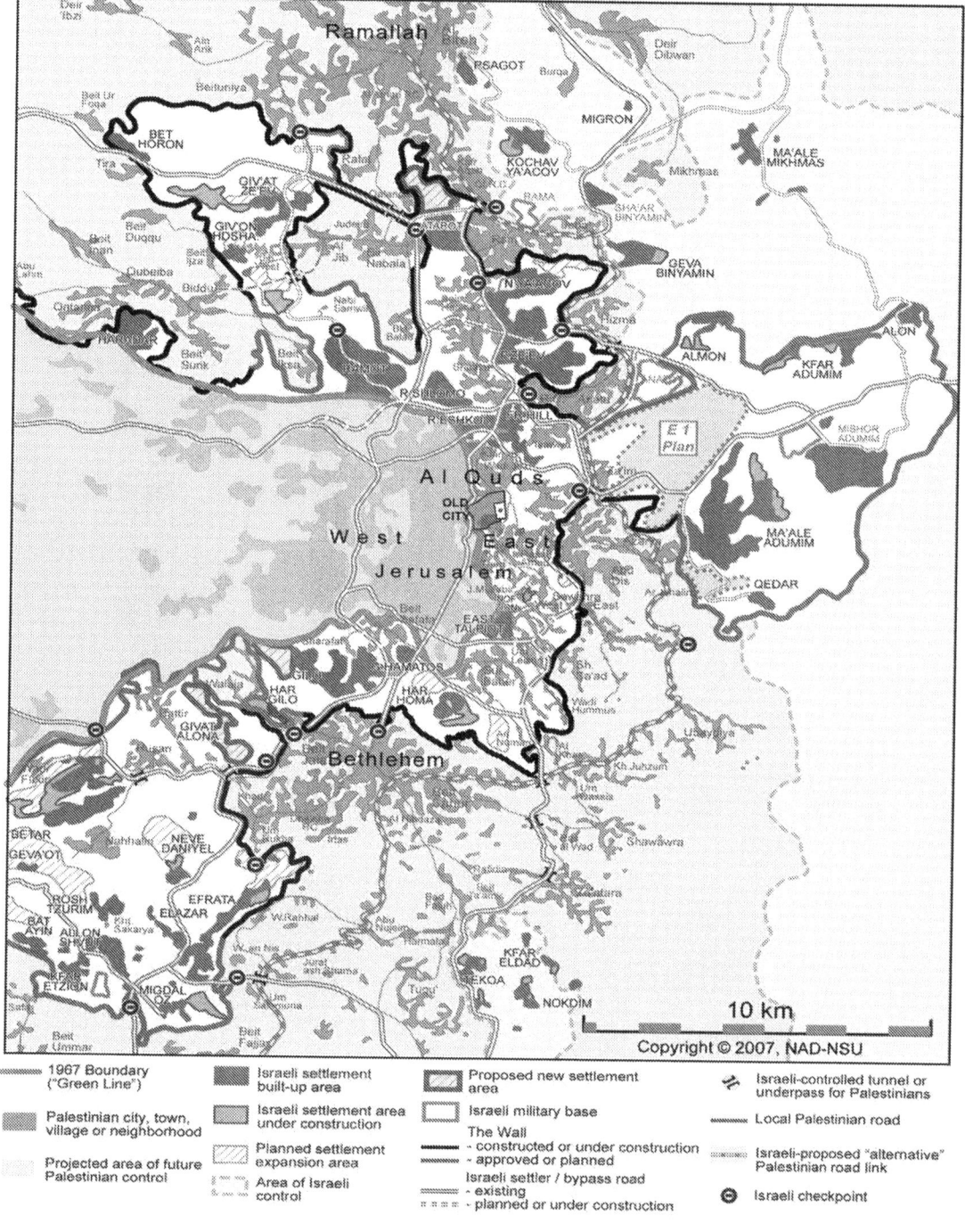

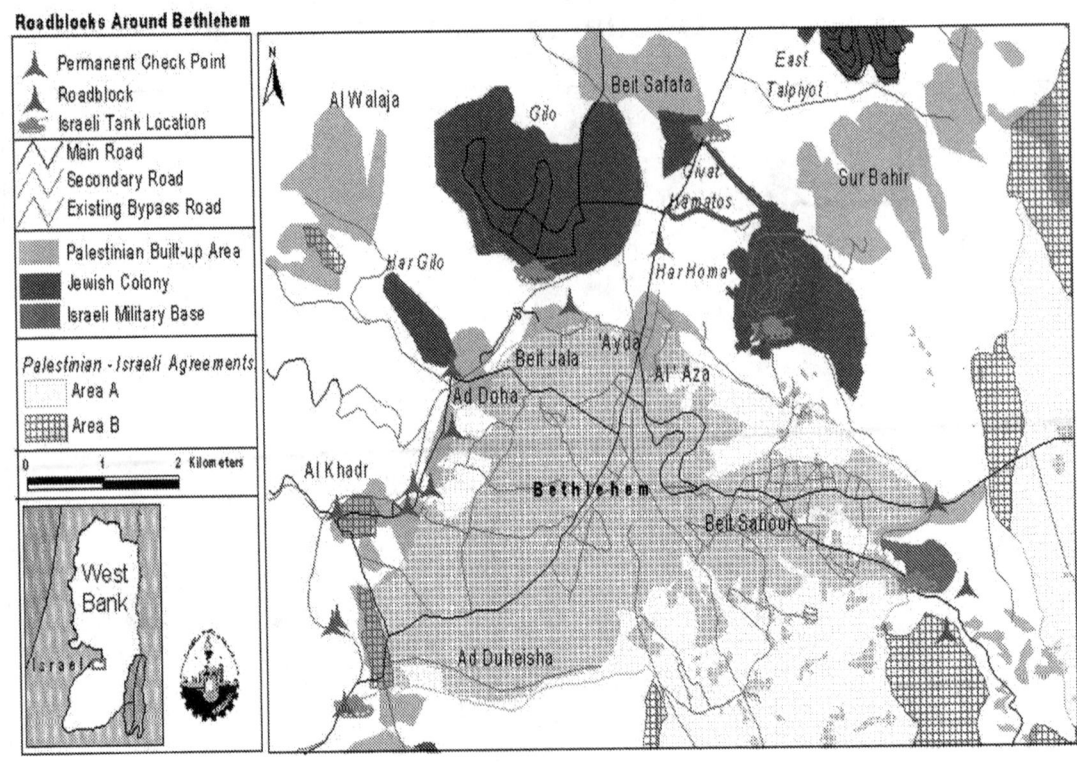

Maps Courtesy of : **NAD-NSU** (PLO Negotiations Affairs Department- Negotiations Support Unit)

PASSIA (Palestinian Academic Society for the Study of International Affiars)

B'TSELEM (The Israeli Information Center for Human Rights in the Occupied Territories)

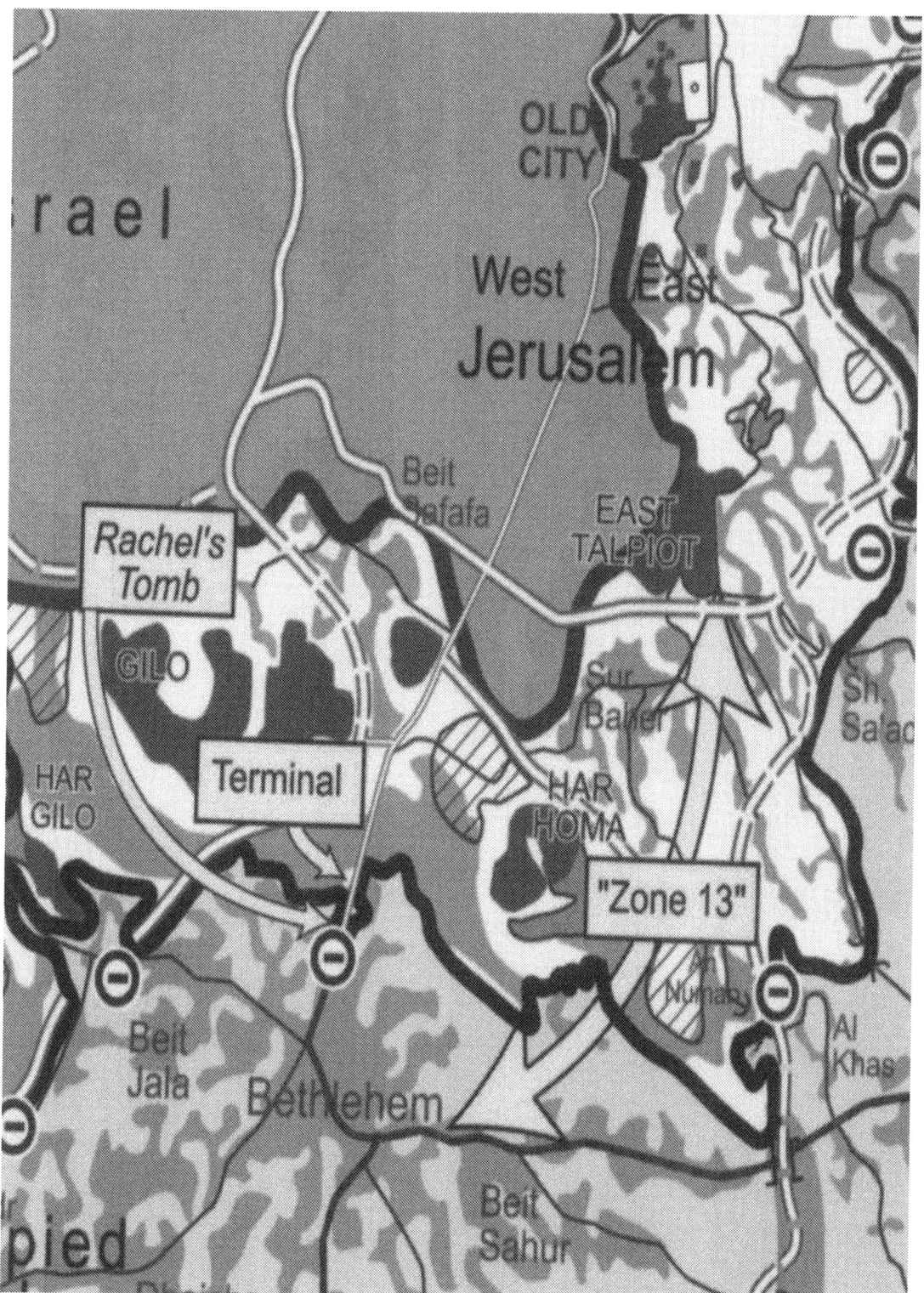

IN HILLARY'S FOOTSTEPS

Eulogy to the Creators of the Apartheid Wall

"[O]ur future here in this country is intertwined with the future of Isarel . . . . I want to start by focusing on our [sic] deep and lasting bond between the United States and Israel.

"Now, these are bonds that are more than shared interests. These are bonds forged in a common struggle for human rights, for democracy, for freedom. . . .[T]hey are rooted in fundamental beliefs and values about the dignity and rights of men and women to live in freedom, free from fear, free from oppression. . . .

"Israel is not only . . . a friend and ally for us, it is a beacon of what democracy can and should mean."

(From Senator Hillary Clinton's comments to AIPAC, May 25, 2005.)

Senator Hillary Clinton has maintained on her website for the past two years pictures taken during her visit to Israel in November of 2005. The website says she is in Gilo, a Jerusalem neighborhood.

Actually, rather than a "Jerusalem neighborhood," Gilo is a settlement started in 1971 by the Government of Israel. After the Six Days War of 1967 Israel confiscated most of the orchards and farmland of the ancient Christian town of Beit Jala, just outside of Bethlehem. What once supported dozens of Palestinian families had become a priority target for illegal annexation, as it was the highest area between Jerusalem and Bethlehem, looking down on both of them. The government of Israel encouraged Jewish citizens and Jewish immigrants to populate the area, using a variety of generous incentives. Gilo now houses 40,000 Jews, mostly religious, 3% of whom speak English -- which must primarily be those immigrants from Brooklyn and Queens who had become fed up with all the restrictions of civilized life in NYC and yearned for the wide open spaces of the lawless Occupied Territories where they could carry weapons and chase the natives, all with Government provocation and support.

The colony of Gilo is one of a series of Jewish settlements intended to separate Jerusalem from the West Bank and at the same time choke to death the Christian city of Bethlehem and its surrounding villages. The remaining built-up part of Beit Jala would look like part of Bethlehem to an outsider, the village being separated from Bethlehem only by Pope Paul VI Street. It has a population of approximately 12,000 and contains centuries-old churches and seminaries. Beit Jala, like Bethlehem, is now on the other side of Israel's Apartheid Wall, the 30 foot concrete wall that Clinton had come to visit and bless.

Beside her in one of the photos on her website are Israeli military officers and politicians pointing out to her the finishing touches being made at that time to the Wall. In her speeches about this visit she has paid special tribute to one of the individuals in her photo, a Col. Danny Tirza. Tirza, a protégé and long-time agent of Ariel Sharon, was the military official who oversaw the Wall's building, and is called "Mr. Fence" in Israel (sections of the "Wall" are double or single electrified metal fences plus "security" zones on either side). While overseeing its construction Tirza also made sure that the Wall at one point meandered well away from the Green Line (the 1948 War's Armistice Line or the boundary prior to the 1967 War) deep into the West Bank, about seven or eight miles, to confiscate additional thousands of acres of Palestinian land and water and also, incidentally, to include the orthodox Jewish colony of Kfar Adumim, where he happens to live with some 2,000 other settlers. He has since retired to that community.

Unlike Pontius Pilate, however, Clinton did not have the sense to wash her hands. Rather, she lavishly praised the crucifixion. This is the 30 foot concrete wall and electrified fence that separates the place where Jesus was born, Bethlehem, from the place where he was crucified, Jerusalem. For two thousand years Christian pilgrims would come to pray at these holy sites. The roads between these two Christian meccas had become dotted with churches that had been built up, destroyed, and built up again over the centuries. Now they face a new threat. Bethlehem itself is becoming a ghost town, with the disappearance of pilgrims and tourists – frightened off by the Israeli Wall, checkpoints, military raids, assassinations, bank closures, discriminatory roads, Israeli scare propaganda, etc.. (See page 95.)

Most Christian tourists still willing to brave the scene now arrive and leave, the same day, on Israeli tour buses, the final knife into the Palestinian tourist industry, run primarily by Palestinian Christians. Economics is never far from the Israeli strategy — when it kills a business in Bethlehem, a Jewish one in Jerusalem or in one of the surrounding settlements benefits. If there were a Home Depot on one side of the road and a Lowe's Home Improvement on the other -- kill the Home Depot, and who benefits?

And Clinton called it good.

Her website quotes her as saying that the Wall will be good for both the Israelis and the Palestinians; that it was not against the Palestinians, but against terrorists. Also, in an echo of the Bush-Cheney lawlessness and disdain for international institutions, she states:

> ***"I've taken the International Court of Justice to task for questioning Israel's right to build the security barrier."***

"I've taken . . . to task . . . " the most august judicial body in the world! What an incredible thing to say.

The World Court, as it is commonly called, was established in 1945 by the Allies, with the United States being the most enthusiastic supporter, as the highest court in the world and intended to help settle disputes among nations. Its 15 judges are highly respected men and women of substantial experience. Its decisions are as reasoned and researched as any court's opinions could be. Yet Hillary, herself a lawyer whose major experiment in practicing law led to many years of bitter litigation and criminal investigations (the infamous "Whitewater" fiasco), has the indecent temerity to brag about taking the court "to task."

Even Bush was not brazen enough to advertise *before* he got into the White House that he intended to put himself and the United States, for the first time in its history, outside the laws of civilized nations. He did, indeed, make that announcement early in his Administration, with the belligerent neo-conservative doctrine of "pre-emptive" or "first strike." According to this new doctrine, we warned the rest of the world that we would attack militarily any nation it we *felt* it were a threat, whether it presented an imminent threat or not, and regardless of whether it had attacked us first. Never before had a President stated that he would use military force except in defense of our country against an actual attack. Former President Carter called it a reversal of 200 years of American foreign policy. Of course that doctrine has since been totally discredited with its first test — the horrendous experiment in Iraq. Hopefully it will disappear with the end of the Bush-Cheney regime. Though if Hillary Clinton is elected President she might feel compelled to hang on to this masculine-sounding doctrine just for the sake of her image.

There is, however, a difference between the Bush-Cheney disdain for international law and that of Hillary Clinton's. The Bush-Cheney position is based on neo-con philosophy. Hillary's, on the other hand, is based simply on money. Her largest and closest financial backers are wealthy American Jews, many of whom had also supported her husband. She will owe them payback if she becomes President. That payback may be to do what Israel has been vainly urging Washington to do, with more and more intensity, almost to the point of hysteria, for the past year – to attack yet another neighbor of Israel, this time, Iran. Certainly wealthy American Jews, given the choice, would be as little inclined as the rest of Americans to ignite another uncontrollable conflagration. But their normal thought processes seem to elude them when it comes to Israel. Whatever Israel wants, Israel gets: right or wrong. If Israel wants to bomb Iran, it must be the right thing to do. They follow Israel. Hillary follows the money.

Israel, the only nuclear power in the region and with a conventional military machine, thanks to the US, that maintains a commanding dominance over all of its neighbors combined, has encountered some rare resistance in Washington as of late. It's provocations for war have been less successful this time around. Of course its Fifth Columnists in the Administration, like the man in charge of formulating Israel policy for the White House, Elliot Abrams, are still vigorously advocating a military solution to their perceived problems with Iran. But the attack dogs are tired and worn out by Iraq. There is hesitancy and ambiguity. There is a step forward, and a step back. But Hillary, on the other hand, will start off fresh. During her political honeymoon she will be able to kill two birds with one stone: pay off her Jewish contributors and at the same time demonstrate, once and for all, that a woman in the White House could be as belligerent and destructive as any man.

Not satisfied with spanking, on behalf of Israel, the world's highest and most respected judicial tribunal, Senator Clinton even seems to suggest that there are so many "shared values" between America and Israel, that, given the chance, we ourselves would have built the same type of wall that Israel is building. This "shared values" concept has become almost a mystical incantation for Senator Clinton. It surfaces sooner or later in all of her speeches to Jewish groups. It showed up, for example, in her remarks to the American Israel Public Affairs Committee (AIPAC) on February 2, 2007:

> *"[As] both Israelis and Americans know so well, a democracy is far more than just holding elections. Democracy has to spring from an active and open citizenry dedicated to tolerance, to respect for differences, to the rule of law, to policies that lift us up, not tear us down as fellow human beings, and to the value of human life. . . . "*

My recent month-long visit to Palestine, partly with a Global Exchange delegation and assisted by a Palestinian tour group, Guiding Star, taught me much about Israeli "values." In a word, they are just plain repulsive.

Even Israeli commentators routinely bemoan the rampant corruption in Israeli politics and its business world (the last five or six prime ministers have all been investigated for financial corruption). Its laws are riddled with discriminatory and racist provisions against it's non-Jewish citizens. Israel's treatment of the millions of Palestinians under one of history's longest military occupations is cruel and mean-spirited. Soldiers who kill and then pump 20 bullets into a 13 year girl for good measure are promoted.

For Hillary Clinton, therefore, to characterize all this barbaric oppression as "uplifting" to the human spirit is truly hallucinatory, or worse.

HALLUCINATORY — In Words: "Shared Values."

Two bedrocks of our form of government are *equality* and *due process*. American democracy would not be recognizable without either of these two basic principles and most Americans would not consider any country to be a democracy without them..

EQUALTIY

Certainly the struggle for equality in the United States has taken a long, torturous and even bloody route from Thomas Jefferson's "We hold these truths to be self-evident, that all men are created equal . . ." to LBJ's Civil Rights Acts of 1964. But today it is universally instinctive in our culture to view with abhorrence any act of invidious discrimination by our government, most particularly any discrimination based on race, religion or national origin. In addition, most people would find offensive such discrimination when practiced by companies or businesses, or even by individuals. And our laws, widely supported by Americans, make most such practices illegal.

In contrast, THE bedrock principle of the Israeli form of government, also widely supported by Israelis, is that all men and women are NOT created equal; that those individuals who profess to be of one religion, namely, Judaism, are to be privileged in almost every manner over all others. There are scores of laws and practices in Israel that enforce this discrimination. One example is that in Israel anyone can refuse to sell or rent property to you because you are a Christian, a Muslim or any religion other than Jewish.

Hillary Clinton can not be unaware that the essential foundation of the State of Israel is the type of religious and racial discrimination that is not only illegal in the US but roundly despised by us Americans. In her desperate pursuit of favor with the Israeli Lobby, she has shamefully, and incredibly for an American Senator, aggressivley acted to aid and abet this Israeli tenet of invidious discrimination. On her official Senate website, maintained by the US Government, is a letter she wrote to the UN, together with other Senators, urging it to grant the Jewish National Fund of the United States general consultative status – something that would allow it to have more influence in UN activities. The letter speaks mostly of the JNF's environmental experience, conforming to JNF's innocent "tree planting" cover story to explain that organization's *raison d'etre*.

What is not mentioned in the letter, however, and the reason the JNF and most other Israeli institutions have been ostracized by international non-profit organizations, is that the JNF is the quasi-government agency used by Israel to exclude Christians, Muslims and Arabs from most of the apartments and houses developed in the metropolitan areas of Israel.

Certainly Clinton knows this. Anyone with the slightest curiosity would learn this fact from a perusal of the entry for the Jewish National Fund on the internet encyclopedia website Wikipedia. I cannot imagine a Senator's staff would prepare such a letter for her to be sent to the United Nations, and then posted on her website, without the Senator being aware of the nature of the JNF. Yet, even while knowing JNF's intrinsic racist purposes and practices, Clinton went out of her way to advocate its cause.

The JNF (I ignore the paper difference between the US branch and its parent in Israel, as the US branch's charter makes it a creature of its parent in Israel and it has always behaved that way) owns about 13 to 15% of the land in Israel, most of it in metropolitan areas. Their land is the most valuable in Israel as it is where 75% of Israelis live. While the JNF was originally founded in the early 20th Century to buy land in Palestine for Jews with donations from Jews in the Diaspora (the "blue boxes"), most of the huge amount of land it now owns was acquired at practically no cost from the Israeli Government in 1950. The land which the Israeli Government gave to the JNF in

1950 had been where the homes, factories, orchards, farms and businesses of the Arabs were located who had been driven out by the Zionist armies before, during and after the 1948 war.

The whole scheme of giving this stolen land to the JNF was intended to allow the Government of Israel to enforce its "Jews-only" discriminatory policies, which it rightly suspected might hinder its efforts to gain entry into the world community, without subjecting itself to charges that it was engaging in such activities itself. The JNF's charter allows it to sell or lease land ONLY to Jews. That convenient arrangement is healthy and alive today. (Incongruously, this malevolent instrument of a foreign government is able to maintain *tax-exempt* status in the US as a *charity* — meaning that you and I indirectly help support this racism.)

Coincidentally, Israeli newspapers in July and August of 2007 are filled with a debate about a bill, overwhelmingly given an initial green light by the Knesset (64 to 16), that expressly confirms the right of the government to continue using the JNF to enforce its discriminatory practices. Billionaire Ronald S. Lauder, then the President of the JNF (now its Chairman), and the recently elected President of the World Jewish Congress, issued a press release in response to that vote expressing his gratitude that the Israel will continue to exclude non-Jews from the lands owned by the JNF. "We are a people linked to our land. Now and forever."

Just as *equality*, therefore, is interwoven into the fabric of American life, in Israel the binding thread of that nation's fabric is racial and religious *bigotry* – "Now and forever."

DUE PROCESS

In America, even a child knows that here a person cannot be arbitrarily arrested or put in jail for years without a trial, evidence presented in open court, a judge to hear both sides and a jury of one's peers to decide the fate of the accused. True, *due process* has taken a beating in recent years from the Bush-Cheney Administration. But the fierce opposition to their "enemy combatant" doctrine, their secret wiretapping and their secret rendition programs attest to the vibrancy of American vigilance for our freedoms.

Yet again, in sharp contrast, stands the State of Israel. Every day the Israeli Army arrests, without warrants or any other judicial procedure, many people around the country and in the Occupied Territories. Death sentences are imposed in secret and carried out by the Israeli military in the middle of the night or in broad daylight. Individuals are executed on the streets or in their beds without warning, much less with any judicial review. Homes are broken into at all hours of the night and their occupants dragged into the street. Ten thousand political prisoners are in jails, most without charges having been brought against them, much less the opportunity to present evidence, be heard in open court or have a judge or jury of their peers listen to their defense.

HALLUCINATORY — In Numbers.

It is difficult to describe in words the enormity of the disconnect from reality that Senator Clinton's elaborate praise for Israeli "democracy" reflects. The character, philosophy and principles, or values, of Israel and the United States could not be more different. Where words fail, perhaps numbers will succeed.

Israel has a population of 5.5 to 7.0 million people, depending on which source one uses and which "Israel" is included. (When it comes to the Israelis, nothing, particularly numbers, is transparent.) I will use the figure of 6.3 million for the purpose of this illustration. The Occupied Territories have a population (not counting the Jewish settlers) of about 4.2 million. Together that is 10.5 million. The United States has a population of 300 million.

From September 28, 2000 to July 23, 2007 one relatively respectable report puts the number of Palestinians killed by the Israeli military at **4,815**. This means that if Hillary Clinton is correct that the US and Israel have the same values, then the United States military would have killed a total of **137,550** people in the United States during the same period. Among the 4,815 Palestinians killed, there were **966 children**, boys and girls under the age of 17. So, if the US were like Israel, we would have killed in that seven year period a total of **27,600 of our children**. Even in so secretive a Bush-Cheney Administration I do not think such an horrendous slaughter would have escaped notice.

Israel is generally considered (again, nothing is transparent in Israel) to have in prison about **10,000** Palestinian men, women and children. Most of these people were arrested without warrants and languish in jails without charges having been brought against them, without trials or evidence presented against them, much less an opportunity to defend themselves. Their only crime, in the system that is Israel, is that they resisted what almost the entire world considers an Occupation that is illegal, and that they sought freedom from oppression and exploitation. These are what are generally called "political" prisoners.

If the United States were so close in spirit to Israel, which Senator Clinton claims is the case, then we would have **285,690** political prisoners in our jails. Again, notwithstanding Guantanamo and the Bush-Cheney secret renditions, I doubt we would have failed to notice the disappearance of close to 300,000 of our fellow citizens.

ARMED JEWISH CIVILIANS

Then there is the startling specter of armed Jewish civilians in the streets, everywhere.

Jerusalem and every city and town in Israel is flooded with heavily armed Israeli soldiers. On some trains they are so numerous that you would think you were in a military camp. Everywhere you turn, there are armed soldiers. Even in the holiest places in Jerusalem, you cannot turn down a street without encountering armed soldiers. Soldiers on foot; soldiers in jeeps; soldiers stopping vehicles and questioning occupants; soldiers peering out from tinted windows in double parked personnel carriers; soldiers attacking you at peaceful demonstrations against the Apartheid Wall.

Yet, along with these soldiers, who one would think were more than enough protection for any imagined threat or risk, there are Jewish civilians everywhere casually carrying their rifles and handguns in open view. A Christian or a Muslim citizen doing the same would be considered a "terrorist" and immediately arrested or executed. In fact, in this society a young Christian or Muslim man cannot go for a quiet walk in his own city – at any moment he can expect to be pulled aside by Israeli soldiers or Jewish civilian "security agents" and interrogated and searched without explanation. I saw that happen a number of times even in Palestinian East Jerusalem.

Can one, in any of this, recognize American values and principles? Hallucinatory, then, is not too strong a term to describe Hillary Clinton's rhapsodies on Israeli "democracy."

SOLDIERS WITH GUNS

HILLARY IN GILO

JEWISH CIVILIANS WITH GUNS

HILLARY IN GILO

HILLARY IN GILO

A CHECKPOINT

A journey going north from Bethlehem, to Jerusalem and then to Ramallah, used to involve a simple and straightforward ride through contiguous communities connected by families, traditions, institutions, businesses and culture. Today, however, one encounters a Jewish-made Kafkaesque maze of giant concrete watchtowers topped with dark and ominous sniper posts, numerous identity checks, impromptu "flying" military checkpoints, temporary and permanent bunker-house checkpoints, turnstiles, questions, identity cards, permits — along with overriding rudeness and meanness – that is, if you are not Jewish. Those Israelis with yellow, or Jewish, plates on their vehicles encounter no obstacles as they glide by the checkpoints, almost as if they did not exist. The rest of humanity, however, coming into Jerusalem must exit whatever vehicle they are in, a cab or a bus, and walk through to the other side because Palestinians are for the most part not allowed to take their vehicles into Jerusalem.

After exiting your vehicle, you walk some distance through a large courtyard where you again experience the uplifting nature of Israel's shared humanity. While walking through the courtyard you are forced to view what must pass for Israeli black humor these days: a large and gaily painted sign on the Wall from Israel's Tourist Bureau that reads: "PEACE BE WITH YOU". (See page 108.) A cruel play on Dante's: "Abandon all hope, you who enter here!" Or is it intended to be a mockery of Christ's message of peace?

Then you enter a modern, plain, low cement building reminiscent of the ill-omened buildings faced by refugees in the old World War II movies, where you go through several turnstiles, baggage checks and hand scanners (for Palestinians with the right "permits"), all the time being observed by cameras and soldiers behind tinted windows in various booths. Off with your shoes and belt, all coins and wallets into the basket, etc., etc., etc. Then when I thought we had finally shuffled through to the Jerusalem side and I was spinning through the final turnstile, some invisible Jewish finger had a final joke to play. The turnstile suddenly froze and I bumped my head against the bars.

We waited patiently. I had learned during my stay in Palestine to take my cue from those around me who had more experience with these humiliating measures. They did not react, so I did not react. Yet there was no apparent reason for the stoppage. There was no group of people ahead of us – the line of Palestinians in front had already been "processed." The building was not crowded. Though this was "in season" there were hardly any tourists, that business having been effectively destroyed by the Israelis. Each of the four or five gates were staffed with Israeli soldiers behind their tinted windows. There was no altercation of any sort to slow things down. Yet we stood and waited in the stifling heat.

Eventually one of the children from the line went up to the front and pushed a button that I had not noticed before. She pressed it again and again. I assume it rang a bell in one of the booths, but I did not hear anything. There was no motion or sound from the Israeli soldiers in their booths. The soldiers, barely more than children themselves, ignored whatever sound that button may have made in their booths and continued to chat with each other, laugh and prattle on the phones, as if the humans milling about just in front of their noses, people being kept from their doctors, schools, offices, churches, relatives, jobs, did not exist. It seemed that at least none of *these* Israelis were the ones that Clinton must have had in mind when she talked about the American and Israeli shared values of justice, equality and what not, all geared to uplifting humanity.

I knew that this expression of the child's annoyance would only feed the cruelty behind those tinted windows. So I shushed her away from the button. What could delight an Israeli border guard more than the fact that he or she was upsetting Palestinians. The girl shyly backed away and went over to her mother further down the line.

Fifteen minutes later a young lady, with one infant strapped to her front and carrying another in her arms, came up to the button. She pressed it again and again, angry and agitated. This time I felt I could not shoo her away. She started to tremble and banged on the gate, again and again. She yelled out something. This time there was a response. A very harsh and loud female voice boomed out over the loudspeakers shouting something several times. The mother backed away and returned to her place in the line, still seething and shaking her head.

The Palestinian mothers and children I was waiting in line with; the old Palestinian fellow trying to get to Jerusalem from Bethlehem to see his doctor; the sober men in suits and ties behind me; the laborers with their lunch bags — none of us could see the benefit of this Wall for the Palestinians, much less how it lifted us up as "fellow human beings." In fact, the one thing that became clear to me during my time in Palestine, was that the Israelis do not consider Palestinians as their fellow human beings, but a plague to be purged from their "Promised Land."

When we eventually did get through, the soldiers and border police in the area outside the checkpoint exit were arrayed about with their automatic rifles at the ready, theatrically alert and menacing, glaring at the stream of sweating and unsettled people, including me, as we hurried to the waiting buses. I was angry and cursing, but knew enough to keep my voice low and only let the soldiers see that my lips were muttering at them – hopefully behavior just below the level that would provoke them. No need to cause more pain to my fellow commuters as we hastened along. I had the luxury of blowing off some steam by making a display. Not much would happen to me with my American passport, and I was not in any rush to go anywhere. But the Israelis would be sure to take their anger out on the Palestinians.

I noticed a fair amount of Ethiopians among the phalanx of armed soldiers glaring at us as we exited. Israel likes to broadcast its "diversity" by posting an inordinate number of Ethiopian soldiers at these checkpoints. And the Ethiopian-Israelis dutifully repay this favor by often being more harsh and unpleasant to the Palestinians than their compatriots. I am sure that on a random selection there could not be this number of Ethiopians in the Army or border police. When I had traveled a few weeks earlier from Tel Aviv to Haifa on trains packed with armed soldiers, there was only a smattering of Ethiopians. Perhaps the Israelis just enjoy the specter of recently arrived immigrants keeping children, whose families have lived here for hundreds of years, from getting to their schools on time. More salt in the wounds of the natives — just another gratuitous gesture to make their lives unbearable so that they will leave.

The Ethiopian Jews, actually, had good reason to be grateful to the Israelis. According to entries in Wikipedia, Israel's rabbis officially recognized certain Ethiopian communities as Jewish in the 1970's but it was not until the great famine in the 1980's did the Ethiopians begin arriving in Israel in large numbers. To save the Ethiopian Jewish communities from starvation Israel mounted huge airlifts in 1984 and 1991, bringing in over 50,000 of the estimated 90,000 Ethiopians who have emigrated to Israel. Their assimilation has been much more difficult than for groups from Europe or Russia, however, because of their color and lack of skills. In addition, most of them were placed by the government in frontier areas of Israel which the Government wanted to develop. But in the military, at least, they have found a hospitable welcome. Hence, the "ultra" attitude of many of those soldiers.

In any event, upon passing this gauntlet I searched for the bus that we had exited before going through the checkpoint. I would recognize mine, even though there were several Arab buses lined up along the road with the same bus number. Most of the Arab buses were old with their characters written on them with a variety of marks and dents, so that few were alike. Yet it was nowhere to be seen. No one else seemed concerned, since it appeared that the buses filled up with whomever came out of the checkpoint first and then went on to Jerusalem. But I had a special reason to want to catch the same bus. Unlike the Palestinians who were just communing on daily trips, I had put my luggage in the rear of that bus.

I eventually boarded a bus going to Jerusalem proper. I was angry and mumbling to myself. I said out loud that it was a good thing that nobody understood English because I would be embarrassing everyone with my language. It seemed, though, that if my fellow passengers did not understand my language, they understood what I felt. Yet most people on the bus seemed to be more amused by my anger than anything else. An episode that had made me furious, was only a routine event for most of the Palestinians. One boy, about 20, broadly smiling, if not laughing, insisted that I sit next to him and by his motions he tried to calm me down. Then a lady across from me, who apparently did understand English, asked in if I was OK. I explained my luggage dilemma. Don't worry, she said, this happens often enough. When we get to the Arab bus depot in East Jerusalem, she advised, just ask them to check the buses as they come in from the checkpoint. I did that, and finally got my two bags and was happy again.

It occurred to me as I saw all those amused faces on the bus, that most Palestinians have adopted a strategy of "going along to get along." This must be the way it is in every military occupation. The Israelis, however, would be fooling themselves if they interpret this complaisant behavior as indicating that their final-solution strategy is actually working. Israelis seem to think that if they kill off or jail enough of the recalcitrants, then the rest would become like sheep. Almost every day you read of one or two Palestinian "militants" killed in an assassination; another killed during an "arrest", and several others arrested to join the 10,000 already in prison. The Palestinian "leaders" are now down to boys about 20 years old, like the boy who took pity on me in the bus. Eventually the Israelis hope to liquidate everyone who stands out, one way or another. Then they will have just people like those on the bus who have come to accept their status and will make no "trouble." This is a phenomenal fallacy. Their dream has no support in the history of military occupations in recent centuries.

A DESECRATED CHRISTIAN CEMETERY

If Senator Clinton on that November day in 2005 had just wandered a little on that stone-littered hilltop in Gilo, as I did in May of 2007, she would have stumbled across some unsettling, at least to me, scenes. (See pages beginning at page 40.) A small desecrated cemetery hidden behind a barbed wire fence and overgrown bushes; remains of demolished stone houses; piles of stones and concrete from bulldozed buildings; ancient terraced orchards callously carved up by roads and fences — the remnants of a previous people that were not yet completely erased.

I was surprised to discover as I got closer to the tombstones that the desecrated cemetery was not Muslim, as was the more common instance in Israel. This one was Christian. It reminds one that the lands taken to establish Gilo by Israel had belonged to the Christian community of Beit Jala, most of which was now on the other side of the Wall – cut off not only from their orchards, but from their doctors, teachers, friends and the jobs they had once had in their nearby Jerusalem, now in another galaxy. One of Beit Jala's cemeteries remained behind, almost entirely hidden off from view at a busy intersection at the edge of Gilo. And the Jews have treated it with the same respect, or rather lack thereof, as they have treated the Muslim cemeteries wherever they were found.

In this cemetery I observed testimonials for the dead in English and Arabic beseeching Christ to have mercy on the souls of wives, husbands, parents, brothers, sisters and children. The cemetery had no sign and it was almost invisible at the busy corner of two new roads built by the Israelis, both exclusively for Jews, one to get to Rachel's Tomb and the Jewish settlements beyond, and the other to get into Gilo proper. There were busy bus stops at the intersection, for the Jews-only buses, and long-haired Israeli youths, some carrying automatic rifles, hitching rides on these exclusive Jewish roads to one of the numerous settlements listed on the bus signs.

The small cemetery had what looked like its own original fence, now rusted and collapsing. That was surrounded by a more recent and more robust fence, with barbed wire at the top. Everything was shrouded by overgrown bushes and weeds. The weeds were a foot tall and the place was forlorn. Most of the tombs appeared to have had their stones violently broken or toppled.

The cemetery had been located at the edge of what had been a terraced orchard in Beit Jala owned by a prosperous family. The ruins of a building from the former homestead still stood nearby, and one could see ancient terraces abruptly terminated by the new roads carved out of the hillside by the Israelis on all three sides.

The U.S. State Department in its "International Religious Freedom Report 2006" noted one instance of vandalism at the cemetery:

> "The phrases 'Death to Arabs' and 'Death to Gentiles' were spray-painted in March 2005 on ten graves in a Christian cemetery in Jerusalem's Gilo neighborhood. Police continued to investigate the matter, but had not made any arrests . . . ."

Eight months later when Senator Clinton was walking around the hilltops of Gilo, she might still have been able to see these uplifting graffiti. That is, if she had stumbled across the cemetery, an improbable event in view of who was escorting her.

The stone tablets contained some names and writings in Arabic. The rest though were of English people and their inscriptions were in English. There was a Joseph Hobson and Rose Holmes; Nora Blackman and her brother Alfred Stevens; O.D. Arnold and Rev. Marcia Dodwell; David Allan Ross and Horsting Walter; Henry James Williams and Ruby Kate McGee.

There buried also was a Violet Barbour, her grave marked by one of the few tombstones not toppled or shattered (page 59). I put her name into Google and learned something about her. Violet must have been deeply involved in the Palestinian communities, particularly with women and the then thriving industry of embroidery. Her enthusiasm for Palestinian embroidery was said to have inspired a famous authority on the craft, Shelagh Weir, to study the Palestinian embroidery industry and its fashions.

Violet was married to an English writer and historian, Nevill Barbour, and both lived in Palestine from the 1920's. He had written a great deal about British and Palestinian affairs and seems to have been strongly pro-Palestinian as well.

Violet's tombstone is relatively new and gives her date of birth, 1903 or 1913, and her date of death, 2000. I was curious why she had decided to be buried in a cemetery that must already have been isolated by the Israelis. But while preparing the photos that I took for this book I noticed for the first time the faint traces of the name on the tombstone behind hers: Nevill Barbour. It seems that notwithstanding the desecration by Jews of this Christian cemetery, Violet wanted to be near her husband who had died in 1974 at the age of 79.

Violet Barbour in her long life in Palestine had collected a large number of Palestinian costumes, particularly during the 1930s, and had helped found the Palestine Folk Museum. Her collection of Palestinian costumes is now housed in the Dar al-Tifl, the Children's House, in East Jerusalem.

The Children's House is a reminder of another remarkable woman, Hindi Husseini. This woman was a member of a pre-1948 prominent Palestinian family and had been working with a Palestinian charity in April of 1948 when she found her destiny. One morning she encountered a host of children at the Jaffa Gate. They turned out to be survivors of a massacre at the nearby village of Deir Yassin that had just occurred. Husseini took them to one of her family's more magnificent mansions and gave them shelter and food. She promptly turned the mansion into an orphanage and then a school. Today there are six buildings making up the complex, and they include a college, dormitory, museum and a cultural center.

These were two very special women, Violet Barbour and Hindi Husseini. I feel certain that their spirits were not pleased with the American politician that was now parading over their graves.

The orphans that were housed at the Husseini mansion had survived the deliberate destruction of their village and the slaughter of the village's men by Jewish terrorists. The village of Deir Yassin had tried to stay neutral during the years of skirmishes prior to 1948 between the incoming Jewish immigrants and those extremist Arab groups trying to keep them out. The village elders, like most Palestinians at the time, saw no threat in the growing immigration of Jews from war-ravaged Europe. There was room, they felt, for everybody. They had repeatedly denied entry into their village to Arab extremists who wanted to set up a military base because Deir Yassin's crossroads location had strategic value. The village elders even entered into a formal agreement with one of the Zionist underground military groups, Haganah, promising neutrality in return for not being molested. They kept their promise, but Haganah did not. This could be viewed as the beginning of a long line of broken agreements, treaties, handshakes and promises that come down to our day. The elders were specifically included among those selected for execution after the village had been captured and burned down by the Zionist forces.

Ironically, Deir Yassin's pacific attitude itself, instead of protecting its people, had been the main cause for the village's demise. While other Palestinian towns and villages had some sort of armed defenders, Deir Yassin had counted on their agreement with Haganah for its safety. When the Jewish terrorists had decided to make an example of one village to terrorize Palestinians in neighboring towns and villages into fleeing their homes, they chose Deir Yassin because its history of neutrality and peacefulness made it an easy target. A number of alternative places were rejected as too dangerous to try to capture. In the end it all worked out as the Jewish terrorists had planned.

All of this occurred even before the British, who had been governing Palestine from 1917 under a League of Nations mandate, had vacated Palestine in May of 1948. There had not yet been any battles between the Zionist forces and the neighboring Arab nations. There was as yet no war, though there were numerous violent clashes as the Zionists continued their efforts to drive the British out earlier rather than later and expand the Jewish settlements. The Zionist plan expressly called for the expulsion of all the Arab inhabitants from their homes in the area of Palestine that had been designated by the United Nations in its "Partition" plan as the new Jewish homeland.

So the Stern Gang (Lehi) led by Menachin Begin and the Irgun, labeled as "terrorists" for years by the British Mandate officials, easily ran over this peaceful town and then executed one to two hundred villagers, all as a warning to the rest of the Palestinians. This was an early version of the ethnic cleansing that Israel continues to this.

GILO — A SICK COLONY

The Jewish colony of Gilo has a website which brags about its unrivaled views of Jerusalem (curiously, it does not mention Bethlehem, whose views in fact are even more stunning). According to its website it is "where heaven and earth meet in more ways than one."

Yet this place had a queer feeling about it. As I walked its clean and well paved streets, with benches and flowers and manicured landscapes, I was reminded of another shiny and well-ordered suburban town. It was in the old movie "Stepford's Wives." Husbands with obstreperous wives would move their families to the suburban town of Stepford. In due course the women would suddenly change from being difficult ladies into obedient, subservient, content and loving wives. I wonder if the creator of Stepford's Wives, Ira Levin, had ever been to Gilo. In any event, you learn in his book and in the movie the secret of this marvelous transformation. The wives had been killed and replaced by programmable machines that looked exactly like them.

Gilo, Stepford, built on violently confiscated land; perched over the "little town of Bethlehem" that is so venerated around the world but now is being methodically strangled to death; permeated with reminders of the recently expelled Palestinian natives — not-so-completely destroyed cemeteries; mysterious stone foundations; sad decrepit walls here and there; remnants of terraced orchards. The place seemed somehow to smell foul with fumes emanating up through the earth from the corpse of a raped culture. The town of Gilo-Stepford, so manicured, clean and sterile, surrounded by those broad new roads that exclude all but their "own" – a formula for a diseased soul that was reflected in the suspicious glances I constantly got on my strolls through that town.

On one visit I was photographing down the valley toward Bethlehem when I was approached by a young man wearing a black shirt and black pants, those give-away wrap around sun glasses and a conspicuous earphone sticking out of one of his ears. Israeli security of some sort, again. I was almost going to lift my camera and take a picture of this ubiquitous inquisitor, when I thought better of it.

"What are you doing?" *Taking photos of the view.* "Why are you doing that?" *I am touring.* "Why are you in Gilo?" *I wanted to see Gilo.* "Where are you staying?" *I am staying in Jerusalem.* "Why are you in Gilo?" *I am touring.* "Where is your family?" *They are back home in the US.* "Why are you here by yourself?" *I am touring, I like to see places.* "Do you have any identification?" *Yes, what would you like to see?* "Give me your passport... Do you have another ID?... Do you have a driver's license?... Wait a minute. Stay (putting his hand lightly on my arm) while I check...."

He spends time on his phone talking to someone in his language. He relays my passport information, the numbers on my New York driver's license. Asks me again what I was doing there. Wants to see the photos I took on my camera. Asks me to delete (I had a digital) the photos of the water tanks and electric power lines. I ask: *"Are the water tanks part of security?"* "Yes. Very important... water tanks. Cannot take pictures of them. Stay away from this area" – as he waved his arms towards several buildings.

It seemed difficult for him to multi-task. He had to listen to whomever was talking to him in his earpiece; he had to keep an eye on me; he had to review the photos in my camera as I flipped thru them on my viewfinder. When he finally got to those photos I had taken of some men incongruously herding sheep through the Gilo streets earlier that day, he got bored and stopped his review. He had missed a couple of water tank photos (see pages 73-74). If any of my readers can determine what is the "security" issue in these photos, please let me know.

Perhaps it was just his general uneasiness about photographing tanks containing water that had been stolen from the Palestinians. Even more than the land confiscated after the 1967 War, Israel has been assiduous in controlling all the *water* in the West Bank. The route of the Wall, for example, was chosen in large part because it includes, on the Israeli side, the underground natural reservoir called the West Aquifer, located in the West Bank, from which Israel eventually obtains about a third of its water supply. In any normal relationship between sovereign states, the water in this aquifer would be a resource of the state in which it is located, like oil or gas, and would be sold to the other state which has a need for it.

Instead, Israel has just glommed on to this natural resource by force, just as it has grabbed the underground water in the other aquifers in the West Bank and the water resources in the Jordan Valley. In addition, while Palestinians in the conquered territories have been severely restricted by Israeli regulations and military forces from digging wells or otherwise accessing the water under their own land, Israel has created a modern, efficient and elaborate water-gathering system for its sole benefit. The result is that Jewish interlopers on plundered Palestinian land are using pilfered water to fill their pools and make their lawns green, while Palestinian farmland becomes parched and barren from the lack of water.

The water situation is so grotesque that it would be funny were it not for the real damage and suffering that it causes. Israel *steals* the water from under the Palestinian lands and then *sells* the filched water back to the Palestinians, and at prices far in excess of what it sells such water to Israelis. When the weather is dry, the water supply to the Palestinians is cut off first so that the settlers could continue to water their lawns and fill their pools. The Palestinians, however, do see some of their water returned to them free of charge, but only as foul and polluted sewage draining off the settlements and onto the Palestinians' orchards and farms. Such is the reality of life under the Occupation. Groups like the Jewish National Fund, which often finances this theft, specialize in obfuscating such reality with effusive praise of the marvels of Israeli "engineering" that have made "deserts bloom." No wonder my Israeli interrogator was nervous just about my presence so near the evidence of the crime.

Eventually I go on my way, but not without another warning of caution from him to stay on the main roads. "Take all the photos you want," he said, "but only from the main streets. Do not do this area," again waving to several buildings, "and do not go off the roads. There are bad people there who would rob and beat you. Also, do not go near the fence or roads along the fence down there (gesturing toward Bethlehem), the Army will shoot you."

He did, however, try to be helpful. He pointed to a nearby hilltop as the best place in Gilo to take photos of Jerusalem and the countryside — and by implication, of the 30 foot concrete Wall so ominously conspicuous just a hundred yards down the valley. I asked him if that was where Senator Hillary Clinton had been a few years ago (see cover and page 88.) He said something about how important she thought this was and how she agreed with it and was concerned about Israel. But no, he had not been there, though that was the hilltop where she was.

The mirage that seems to be at the center of the soul of the Gilo community was no better expressed than in the rows of short concrete walls I saw along many of the streets in Gilo (page 76). These 6 to 8 feet concrete structures were gaily painted with fanciful drawings. This mini-Apartheid Wall seemed to have been erected either to protect the residents of Gilo from rifle fire from the angry expelled former residents of Beit Jala down the valley or to hide views of the real 30 foot Apartheid Wall, with its watchtowers topped by tinted glass circular enclosures housing the ever watchful Israeli snipers. To the residents of Gilo it must have been difficult to tell who was being watched and who was being imprisoned.

YET ANOTHER JEWISH OUTPOST

On another day trip to Gilo I noticed that the Jews were expanding the Gilo settlement (page 146). There seems to be a crudely constructed outpost consisting of a series of ugly trailers going up just next to some Crusader-era ruins at the edge of Gilo. The Government, as usual, is a complicit party as new roads are being constructed and sewer and water pipes installed and electric lines strung out. I noticed that there was even municipal bus service running to this new outpost.

I could not tell how much of the Crusader-era buildings, which had survived for a thousand years, partly from benign neglect and partly because they had been converted by Palestinians for their own use, had already been bulldozed by the Israelis. But from the huge mounds of stones and other rubble scattered at various locations around these ancient structures, it appears that the remaining buildings are on their way to early extinction as well. The Israelis seem intent on erasing every trace of the people that they had expelled.

CONCLUSION

Fakery and uneasiness were mixed in equal parts in the colony of Gilo, and it must be something like that in all the other colonies in the West Bank and the Golan Heights. A fakery that has also become part of Hillary Clinton's Presidential stump speeches to Jewish audiences:

> *". . . respect for differences, to the rule of law, to policies that lift us up, not tear us down as fellow human beings, and to the value of human life."**

*10,000 political prisoners.
*4,815 Palestinians, including 966 children, killed in less than seven years.
*Christians, Muslems: not allowed to buy or rent in most areas of Israel. Roads restricted to Jews. . . .

SCENES FROM THE CRIME CALLED GILO

A portion of Route 60 near Bethlehem.

Before the Israelis captured the West Bank in 1967, it was an easy commute for Palestinians traveling on Route 60 from Hebron in the south, up to Bethlehem, then to East Jerusalem and up to Ramallah. Now the trip is either impossible for many Palestinians without the correct Israeli-issued pass or identity card, or is filled with peril and delay. Even a properly "documented" Palestinian driving on Route 60 must endure numerous checkpoints and never knows what restrictions the Occupying Army may have ordered on any particular day — from limits on the hours of use by Palestinians to a total prohibition. Jews, however, move about freely on Route 60, with no worries regarding restrictions or stops and searches.

Road signs on Route 60 point to new Israeli settlements on Jews-only bypass roads. Many older signs that had pointed to Palestinian villages and towns off Route 60 have been blacked out or removed by the Israelis, with either the exits to those towns now barricaded or their locations simply made invisible for travelers on Route 60.

Not surprisingly some angry dispossessed Palestinians from time to time take pot shots at the Israeli cars racing by on Route 60 to the new Jewish settlements. In response the Israelis have fortified many sections of Route 60 with protective concrete walls, further isolating the Palestinians on either side as the road traverses the West Bank. On bridges, where the walls would be too heavy (as in the photos here), the Occupying forces have erected armored screens in their stead.

These photos are of Route 60 as it approaches Gilo and Har Homa (taken from Gilo), with connections to the construction marvel called the "Tunnels Highway" for the exclusive use of Jews and foreigners going to "Rachel's" Tomb in Bethlehem. There the Israelis have carved out another area of Bethlehem, evicting or entombing neighboring Palestinians, to create an enclave around "Rachel's" Tomb, preparing for Jewish occupation.

The Palestinians who can still find humor in their souls are amused at all the efforts being made by the Israelis about this particular piece of earth, going back to 1905 when Sir Moses Montefiore of Britain purchased the site from the Ottoman regime and built the present day tomb. The version of the story I heard from some locals is that this had been just another pile of stones in the late 19th Century until a Palestinian huckster set up a souvenir shop next to it and announced that it was the burial place of Jacob's wife. Some Jewish Scholars place Rachel's burial in northern Jerusalem. Others admit that they have no idea where this mythical figure may have been buried. But today's Israelis have found it convenient to believe that it is located in the heart of a Palestinian neighborhood, justifying the construction of one more cancerous Jewish settlement.

As you travel on Route 60 from Jerusalem to Bethlehem, just before Bethlehem you pass two fortress-like settlements high on the hills, Har Homa to the left and Gilo to the right. The signs above are at Gilo, where the "Tunnel" takes Jews only to Rachel's Tomb and the Jewish Settlements beyond, by-passing Bethlehem.

HILLARY IN GILO

The photographs in color would show that all the license plates on these vehicles are yellow, indicating for the most part that they are Jewish and are allowed to use the by-pass roads without molestation.

As one comes to the Gilo area, you notice a high fence on the right and the remnants of a building. Upon closer inspection it appears that the building, now in ruins and covered with graffiti, had been at the center of the Palestinian orchards of Beit Jala that the Israelis confiscated to create the settlement of Gilo.

Not far beyond the fence, the ruined building and the remaining terraces, are the townhouses of Gilo. Why these few remnants have been allowed to survive and were not bulldozed like the rest of the confiscated area is not clear.

Not only are the roads intended for Jews only, but so are the buses and bus stops as well. Though all the signs, and even the graffiti, are in Hewbrew or English, and obviously intended for Jews only, I did see some Arab buses stop here.

Bus signs on the restricted road f outside Gilo heading towards Rachel's Tomb. Destinations are Jewish settlements.

KIRYAT ARBA located 9.5 miles into the West Bank from the Green Line. Founded in 1972 and had apopulation of 6,819 as of 2005. This colony will be on the Palestinian side of theSeparation Wall as it is now planned.

GUS H ETZYON is the name of a group of settlements south of Bethlehem.

METZAD Established in 1983 and located in the west Bank but near the Green Line. It is included on the Israeli side of the Wall and in 2005 had a population of 431 people.

EFRATA 1980, 4 miles into West Bank, on Israeli side of Wall; 7,428 people.

This is the rather unattractive intersection of Route 60 and the road into Gilo. The fence that we saw along Route 60 continues around into this intersection.

The fence is topped with barbed wire and seems to serve as a bulletin board and a location for advertising posters. A casual passerby would not notice anything beyond the fence and wild shrubbery.

   A closer look beyond the fence reveals a small portion of what must have been a huge orchard and farm. The terraces have obviously not been cultivated for a long time and have fallen into ruin. There are mounds of debris and stones, as if from demolished buildings and terrace walls. Again, beyond these ruins which are carefully fenced in on all sides, rise the buildings of Gilo.

HILLARY IN GILO

Probing and peering beyond the fence that was topped with barbed wire and Israeli flags, I came upon a startling discovery. A portion of the ruined orchard was itself enclosed within an old fence that had a main metal gate and a stone side entrance. Within that area I thought I saw what appeared to be gravestones.

HILLARY IN GILO

I got myself beyond the outside fence and went down what appeared to be the main entrance to this graveyard.

I had read Meron Benvenisti's book, Sacred Landscape, which described the hundreds of Muslim holy places destroyed or desecrated by the Israelis, both in Israel and in the Occupied Territories. I had also just seen the disgraceful condition of the great Muslim cemetery at Independence Park in West Jerusalem. The Israeli Government has bulldozed over and built upon most of that cemetery and even prohibits Muslims from tending to the graves of their families, though it obviously allows vandalism of every sort.

So as I walked down this path toward the dilapidated iron gates, I was not going to be surprised if I discovered that the Israelis had despoiled yet another Muslim cemetery.

The broken headstones, the overturned gravestones, the weeds and the pieces of headstones thrown about everywhere -- these were what I was ready to find. But then I suddenly noticed that some of the headstones bore Christian crosses. As I examined the inscriptions more closely, I was amazed to learn that this was a Christian cemetery that the Israelis had wasted. There were inscriptions in Arabic and English.

JALIL IRANI

HAMMIE J. IRANY
1894 - 1973

50

RUBY KATE MC GEE
Born London 9 Nov. 1892 [?]
Died Jerusalem 13 Oct. 1980

The gravestone at the top, left, is that of O.D. Arnold (see next page); at the top, right, is one inscribed in Arabic and the bottom, broken headstone is that of the Rev. Marcia A.B. Dodwell.

*IN LOVING MEMORY
OF
O.D. ARNOLD*

*HE WAS KILLED IN THE EXECUTION
OF HIS DUTY
ON
MAY 22nd 1948*

*ALL THEY THAT ARE TRUE OF
HEART SHALL BE GLAD*

Arnold's headstone looks like it had been broken in half at one time and then later repaired hastily, as the lines at the break are clearly visible.

His being "killed in the execution of his duty" reminded me that the Zionist forces trying to eliminate the Arabs from Palestine by terror tactics had been killing not just Arabs but also the British who had governed Palestine since World War One. The Jewish underground fighters, many of whom had previously been trained and armed by the British themselves to help suppress uprisings by the Arabs in the late 1930's, had now turned on their former allies and were assassinating British officials.

One of their more notorious acts was the blowing up of the King David Hotel on July 22, 1946, then serving as the Headquarters of the British Mandate Government. The massive blast killed 92 people and wounded 58. The King David slaughter had been carefully planned after approval by the head of the Jewish Agency, which was coordinating the Zionist forces, David-Ben-Gurion, later to become Israel's first Prime Minster.

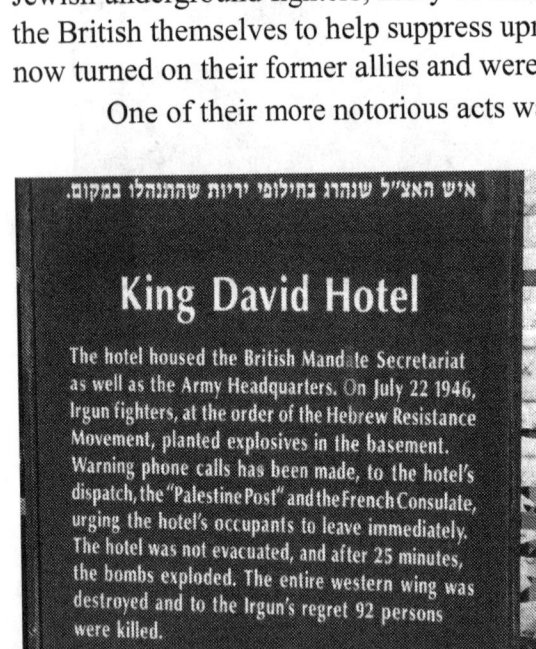

Today the sumptuous lobby and meeting rooms of the King David Hotel (photo left) is stuffed with huge photos, murals and paintings celebrating the great moments in

Zionism's history. The almost kitsch decorum even includes a Hollywood-type walk in the lobby with the names of famous visiting celebrities inscribed on brass plates on the floor. The Hotel serves as a meeting place for the high and mighty in the Jewish world when they are in Jerusalem and often hosts meetings between Israeli officials and foreign dignitaries.

Israel has placed a plaque on the fence outside the Hotel which blames the victims of the Irgun's bombing for their own deaths because they had stubbornly refused to run out of their Headquarters after supposedly getting a warning from the terrorists. "The entire western wing was destroyed and to the Irgun's regret 92 persons were killed."

Four months after O.D. Arnold was killed, and then buried in Beit Jala, the Zionist terrorists would ambush the motorcade of Count Folke Bernadotte of Sweden and kill him. Bernadotte had been sent by the UN as its first ever mediator to help stop the war between the Arabs and the Jews. He quickly established a truce (that was to die with his own death, as intended). Bernadotte came from the royal family of Sweden and had a distinguished diplomatic career, gaining heroic stature for his part in rescuing thousands of prisoners, including many Jews, from German concentration camps near the end of WWII.

(Photo: Britannica Concise)

An eyewitness, General Aage Lundstrom, described how the Count had arranged with the Jewish forces earlier that day to meet Doctor Bernard Joseph, the Jewish Military Governor of that part of Jerusalem then under Jewish control. Bernadotte's unarmed and unguarded two car motorcade passed from the neutral zone, then thru the Arab zone and then over the Arab-Jewish lines and into the Jewish zone without incident. But once into the Jewish zone its progress was suddenly blocked by a Jewish Army jeep filled with armed men in Jewish Army uniforms. Immediately one of the armed men from this jeep went directly to Bernadotte's car. "I took little notice of this because I merely thought it was *another checkpoint* [emphasis added]." But this man in the Jewish Army uniform went right to the back of the car where Bernadotte was sitting, put a Tommy gun through the open window and shot Count Bernadotte and Colonel Serot of France at point blank range, killing both.

The assassination, it was learned years later, had been approved by the leader of the Stern Gang, Yitzhak Shamir, another future prime minister of Israel, in order to scuttle Bernadotte's peace plan which had been gaining traction. The Zionists felt that they needed more time to consolidate their gains. No one was ever charged with this crime, though all the leading figures on the Jewish side knew exactly what had happened and who was involved. Indeed, the man who had shot Bernadotte, Yehoshua Cohen, later worked as Ben-Gurion's personal bodyguard.

Thus Israel has the dubious distinction of being the only nation in the world (so far) which murdered a UN official sent by the Security Council to mediate a dispute.

It seems that not much has changed in 60 years.

Even with the extensive Israeli military censorship of their press, I can still read each day in the online Israeli newspapers, primarily in the <u>Haaretz Daily</u> and the <u>Jerusalem Post,</u> about Israel's terror tactics against the people of Gaza, punishing them collectively, to get them to give up one of their remaining forms of resistance to the oppressive occupation, shooting rockets from north Gaza into the border region with Israel. I read also about daily raids in the middle of the night into Palestinian towns and villages, particularly in and around Nablus and Jenin. People, who have secretly been put on a "wanted" list by someone in Israel, are hunted down like animals, kidnapped, arrested or killed. Anyone wandering near the Fence or the Wall or seen around a rocket launcher is shot, with no second thought given to it — resulting in a host of innocent people being killed, including young men trying to crawl into Israel to find work; children playing ball near the Fence or Wall; children playing tag near spent rocket launchers or scavenging for pieces of metal to sell.

Thrust prematurely into life by the sharp instruments of terror and assassination, Israel has grown into no more than a moral pygmy, endlessly feasting upon more and more terror and assassinations, but never being satisfied.

REV. MARCIA A.B. DODWELL

MURIEL E. PRESCOTT 1909 - 1986

To the Memory of
HARRY RAMNARINE, Jr.
Son of Seeromanie & Harry
Born 12 August 1972
Died 19 August 1972
OH SON THOUTHOU CAME
TO US
BUT COULD NOT STAY
MAY GOD GIVE PEACE TO
HIS SOUL

Our Dear Beloved Brother

JOSEPH HOBSON

FallAsleep in Christ
1904 -- 7-12-1986

Thou shall call
and I will answer thee

DAVID ALLAN ROSS
6.8.1904   4.2.1984
of Milngavie Scotland
& Wolverhampton

Jesus said: "I am the resurrection and the life, he who believes in me though he die, yet shall he live."
John 11:23

ANDREW CHARLES COLLETT
March 25, 1966
July 23, 1995
Resting in the land
and near the people
that he loved.

*In Memory
Of Our Dear Son
STEPHEN ROBERT
VIDLER
Born   28 January 1952
Died   7 February 1981
TOO PRECIOUS
IN LIFE
          TO BE FORGOT-
TEN IN DEATH
          R.I.P.*

NORA BLACKMAN
12 Feb 1907
17 April 1989

and

ALFRED STEVENS
Her Brother
16 Nov 1913
17 April 1990

"WE'LL MEET AGAIN"

JOHN DEAN
5.3.1923 New Zealand
6.1.1998 Jerusalem
FAITHFULL SERVANT
OF THE LORD

HE LOVED THE PEOPLES
OF THE MIDDLE EAST

Houses of Gilo just beyond the cemetery.

Proceeding up the road into Gilo, following the fence which encloses the triangle of the cemetery and the remaining ruined orchards.

Looking back down their main street, that is the other Jewish settlement of Har Homa across Route 60. Together they straddle Route 60 like huge vultures.

I often encountered piles of stone and rubble, apparently from the destroyed Palestinian buildings.

This is an example of the Jewish settlers converting one of the confiscated Palestinian homes for their own use.

These are the water tanks that my interrogator was so concerned about.

This is a curious street. The road suddenly becomes unpaved and desolate for the length of only a street. Cetain signs have been removed and there appears to be warning signs of some sort in Hebrew. Then there are two old buildings down that street with a Palestinian woman walking into one of them.

For some reason this sole Palestinian building has been left intact with what appears to be Palestinian residents, right in the middle of Gilo.

For a while after the expulsion of the Palestinians and the construction of this Jewish settlement, Palestinians from the area of Bethlehem and what was left of Beit Jala across the valley would shoot randomly into Gilo. Not surprisingly the confiscation and dispossession had left many angry people in their wake.

Over this period of time there were a number of Gilo residents injured by the shooting, but no deaths. In response the Israeli Army destroyed a good number of buildings in Bethlehem and Beit Jala with motar fire and bulldozers, killed a dozen or so Palestinians, men, women and children, and then erected stone barriers along one or two streets that faced the direction from which the shooting had come. Then they decorated thses barriers with some fanciful paintings.

I suppose these paintings are intended to help the residents of Gilo forget how they got there in the first place; or that there were angry people out there -- and for good reason.

HILLARY IN GILO

HILLARY IN GILO

HILLARY IN GILO

On the other side of these delusional drawings the Israelis have turned Beit Jala's former orchards into a no-man's wasteland all the way down the hillside and right up to the houses and churches of Bethlehem. One wandering anywhere near this complex of security roads, ditches, cameras and electrified fences runs the risk of being shot by snipers stationered everywhere. Bethlehem in the distance is thus being choked to death.

It was from about this vantage point in the destroyed orchards of Beit Jala where Senator Hillary Clinton in November of 2005 viewed the wall then being constructed, and blessed it.

Clinton website photo (top) and AP photo (bottom). November 13 - 15, 2005.

APF photo

So proud of their work.

"See," he seems to be saying to the attentive Senator, "if they get over that, we still have time to shoot them."

AP photo

When Senator Clinton was on that hilltop in the stolen lands of Beit Jala the Wall, the parallel security roads, the watchtowers, the elctrified fences and the no-man's sterile zones had not yet been completed.

The ancient churches of Bethlehem and Beit Jala can be seen, then and now, beyond the Wall.

The hardships, separations and economic disaster for the Christian towns of Bethlehem and Beit Jala were never mentioned in her November 13, 2005 press conference on this hill, only the "sacrifices" the Israelis were making to protect themselves against terrorists.

Even as of this writing, her Senatorial website still portrays her visit to this international crime scene in 2005 as a singular event for which she remaind very proud.

The strangulation of Bethlehem and Beit Jala.

The churches and mosques surrounded by the Israeli Apartheid Wall.

    Imagine the cruelty of the mentality it takes to separate families like this, to put people on one side and their relatives on the other; to separate children from their schools; patients from their doctors; parishioners from their churches; merchants from their customers; farmers from their fields -- every twist and turn of this Wall means pain and suffering for the affected Palestinians. Yet, look again at the faces on the cover of this book -- the architects seem delighted with their work.

    It is the same story over the hundreds of miles of this ugly wall and fence. Not one Israeli is inconvenienced, while tens of thousands of Palestinians are devastated, as the Wall and Fence sit atop additionally stolen Palestinian lands.

The Wall, as in this photo of the Wall at Bethleheml, becomes a "fence" along certain portions of the route. The fence is electrified with enough electricity to shock a person to death if he or she touches it. The fence itself is bordered by a "sterile" zone around it, usually two parallel roads. Sometimes the parallel roads themselves have additional fences on either side of them. The Israelis seem to use the words "security," "sterile" and "military" zone interchangeably. In any case you get shot if you wander into it. The following are examples of the "fence" from another section of the barrier.

CHECK POINTS.

Getting from one to the other side of the Wall dividing Bethlehem and Jerusalem is not a simple task for any non-Jew. One goes through metal checks and baggage searches, questions, ID and "pass" or "permit" verifications, hand scans, etc.

A passport from the US usually guarantees a clean walkthru, though not always. But if you are a Palestinian, even if you have lived in Jerusalem from before the Zionist armies had marched into the City in 1948, it is not an easy thing to do, if it can be done at all.

Arriving by bus to the checkpoint between Jerusalem and Bethlehem, you are told that if you are Jewish, just proceed this way without molestation. If you are not Jewish, then please enter the building for processing. The small buses in the photo on the right, the "Arab" blue and white buses, are lined up waiting for their passengers to pass through the "processing" in the checkpoint building.

HILLARY IN GILO

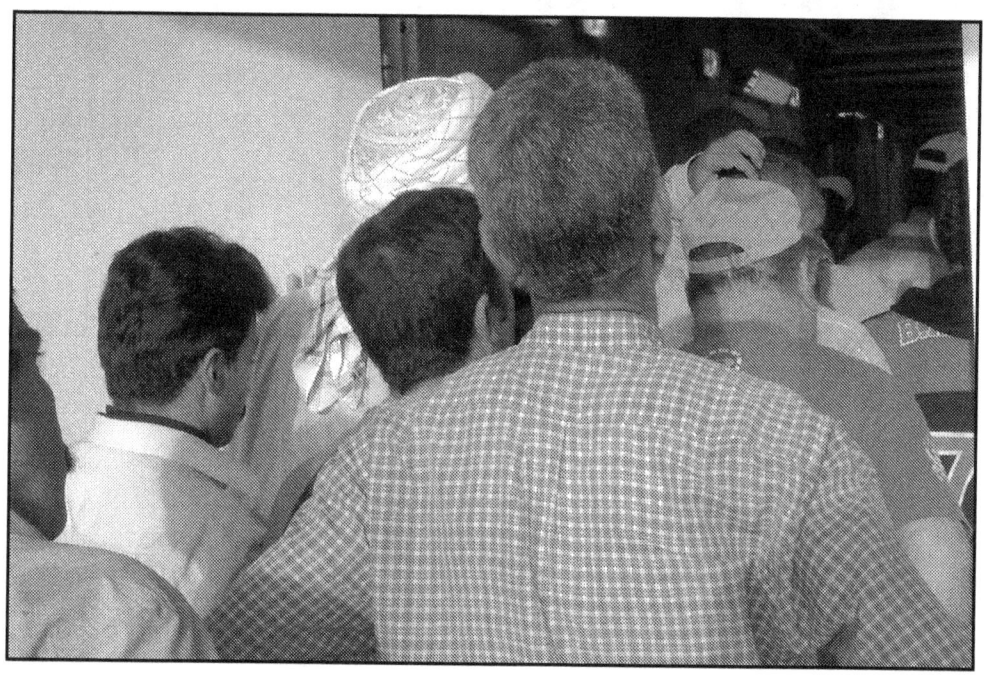

HILLARY IN GILO

Then, when you finally get through all these degrading procedures, you enter the courtyard of the checkpoint between Jerusalem and Bethlehem. There you are confronted with this sign. It stands admist the electirifed fences and barbed wire. It made my blood boil. Such mockery and effrontery to the dignity of those people who have just been beaten up and humiliated by the armed Occupation Forces.

The checkpoint at the other end of Jerusalem toward Ramallalah is not any better. The Palestinians call it the Qalandia checkpoint after its location. The Occupying Forces call it the Atarot checkpoint. But the mockery and cruelty are the same.

HILLARY IN GILO

> **WELCOME TO "ATAROT" CHECK POINT**
> YOU ARE NOW ENTERING A MILITARY AREA. TO MAKE YOUR TRANSIT EASY AND TO AVOID UNNECESSARY DELAY FIRST READ THESE INSTRUCTIONS AND THEN OBEY THEM.
> DO NOT ENTER CARRYING ARTICLES MADE OF METAL OR OBJECTS DECLARED FORBIDDEN BY THE AUTHORITY.
> PREPARE YOUR DOCUMENTS FOR INSPECTION.
> YOUR DOCUMENTS MUST BE PRESENTED AT EACH INSPECTION POINT.
> COATS MUST BE REMOVED.
> PERSONS REFUSING TO FOLLOW INSPECTOR'S OR SIGNPOSTED INSTRUCTIONS WILL NOT BE PERMITTED TO COMPLETE THEIR TRANSIT.
> WE WISH YOU A SAFE AND PLEASANT TRANSIT.
> May you go in peace and return in peace!

The mockery continues:

"We wish you a safe and pleasant transit."

"May you go in peace and return in peace."

Palestinian passengers are required to exit the bus, walk to these barracks, and subject themselves to interrogation and searches as they travel from one of their own towns to another.

Much further north, the facilities at the notorious Huwwara checkpoint at Nablus, where the Occupying Forces make no pretense of civility as the area is off-limits to most foreign observers. The Palestinians trying to get in and out of Nablus are treated like cattle in pens.

Cars and buses must stop at one end of this ever extending area well outside the city, passengers must get out, walk to the other end, go through interrogation and searches, then obtain transportation in another car or bus on the other side.

Coming back from shopping at Ramallah. Everyone must carry their things along this path, from one side of the checkpoint to the other.

You are returning to your own home in Nablus. You had been allowed out to visit relatives in another town, or doctors or stores in Ramallah. Now you carry everything to a machine where the agents of the Occupying Forces poke and inspect the bags and boxes hanging from your arms.

Then you enter these pens, recently "improved" with corrugated metal roofs that only intensify the heat of the sun and make the long wait in line even more miserable. Finally you get your turn to

HILLARY IN GILO

ACROSS TO THE PRISONERS' SIDE OF THE APARTHEID WALL.

Entering into Bethlehem you immediately see the economic and social effects of the Wall. The buildings on either side of the gate are shuttered. Bethlehem's "Main" street, Hebron Road, is deserted.

Israeli snipers and snoopers, with cameras, binoculars and rifles, spy upon the residents of Bethlehem night and day from behind the tinted windows of their towers.

Businesses that once prospered by selling to tourists on a busy Hebron Road, now face a 30 foot concrete wall with Israeli soldeirs and cameras posted in towers looking down on them.

Looking the other way down Hebron Road, away from the Wall. On the right is the Jacir Palace Hotel. Opened in 2000 after millions invested, it stands almost empty.

I found that Bethlehem's hotels and inns were all pretty empty, with the best hotels even refusing guests because it was not worth while for them to operate with just a few guests. That was the case I believe with a couple of the Francisan residences I tried at the center of Bethlehem at Manger Square. But I was lucky to get a luxurious room at the Pilgrim Residence of the Moscow Patriarchate, just off Manger Square on Milk Grotto Street. Most of the institutions and other residences on Milk Grotto Street are operated by the Franciscan.

I stayed at this Russian Residence for a week, many days being the only guest in this fabulous, perhaps 100+ room, hotel. I paid about $50 a day, including meals and full services. I suspect the Moscow Patriarchate subsidizes the Residence. One day I noticed a busload of pilgrims had arrived, for two days, and they were all Russian.

Later, when I traveled to Nablus, I found the same conditions. Empty hotels, though friendly and generous services.

Here are some photos of the Russian Pilgrim Residence on Milk Grotto Street.

Back on Hebron Road at the entrance of Bethlehem, it is not difficult to understand why tourists would not want to stay in Bethlehem --

The Israeli tower -- treated with less than respect on the Bethlehem side.

HILLARY IN GILO

Some Palestinians have used the concrete walls of the prison put up by the Israelis as blackboards to smuggle out their messages to the Israelis and to the world.

These are cries and shouts of definace foremost, but also of hope and some are pleas for help to a seemingly deaf human race. All along the many miles of concrete walls one can find these tokens of resistance.

Here is a sample from the people of Bethlehem and their neighors.

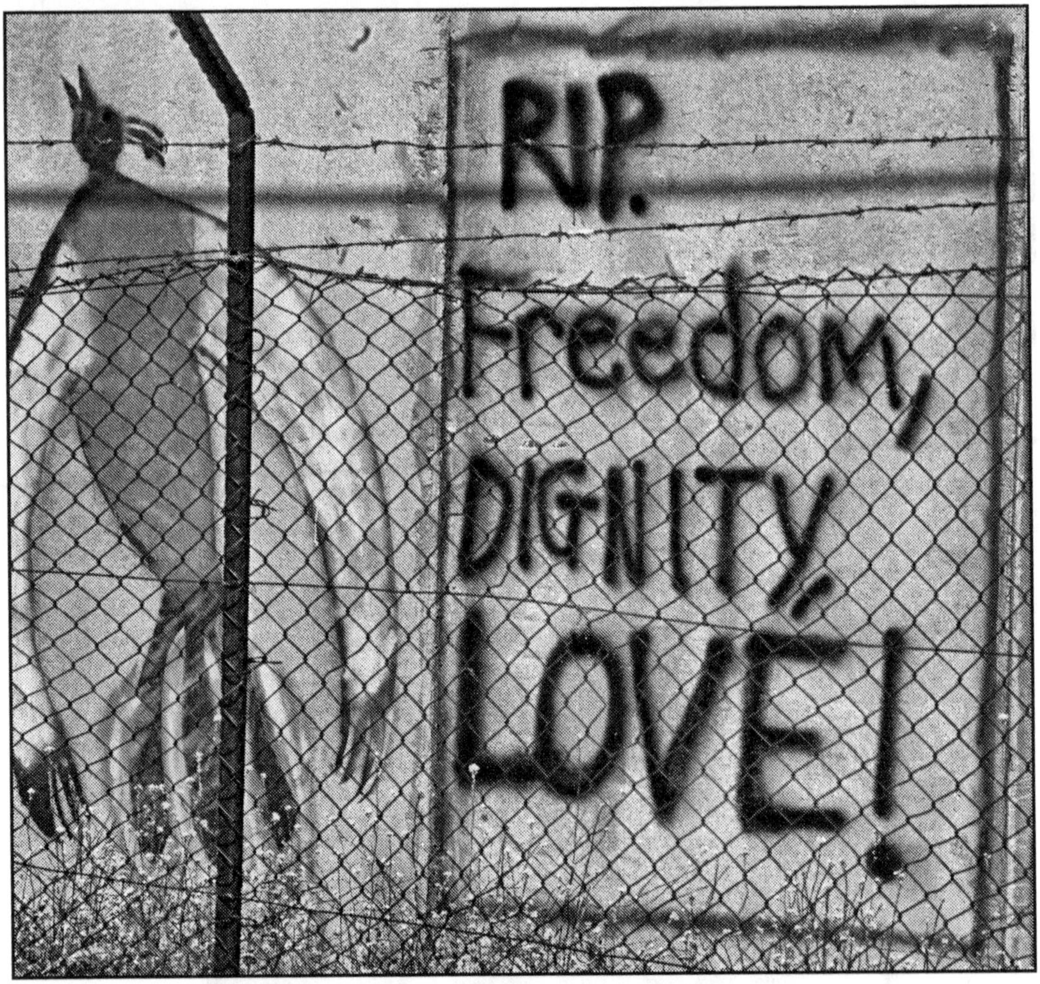
R.I.P.
Freedom,
DIGNITY,
LOVE!

Fuck occupation

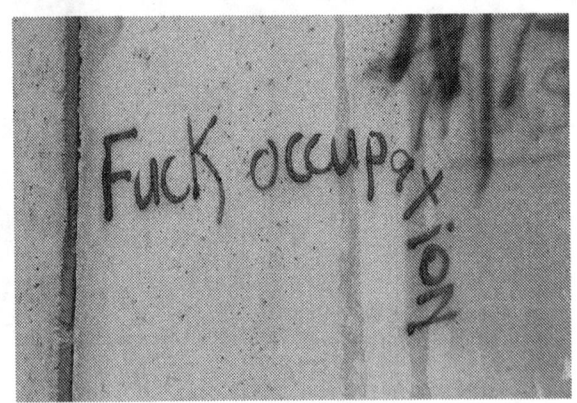

HILLARY IN GILO

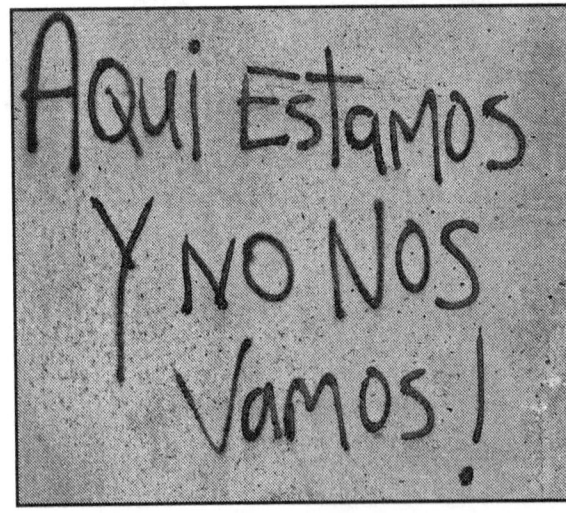

HILLARY IN GILO

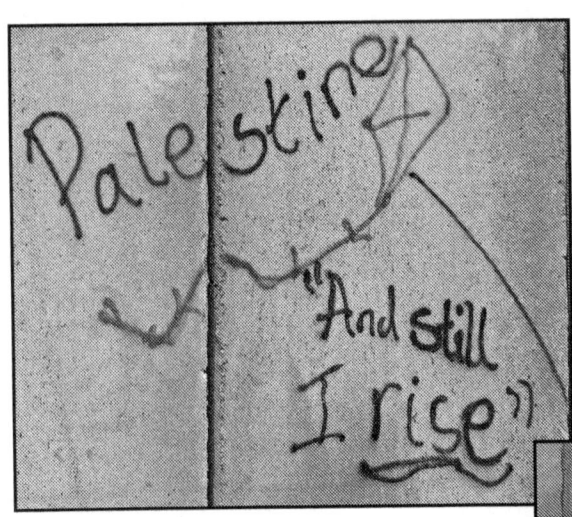

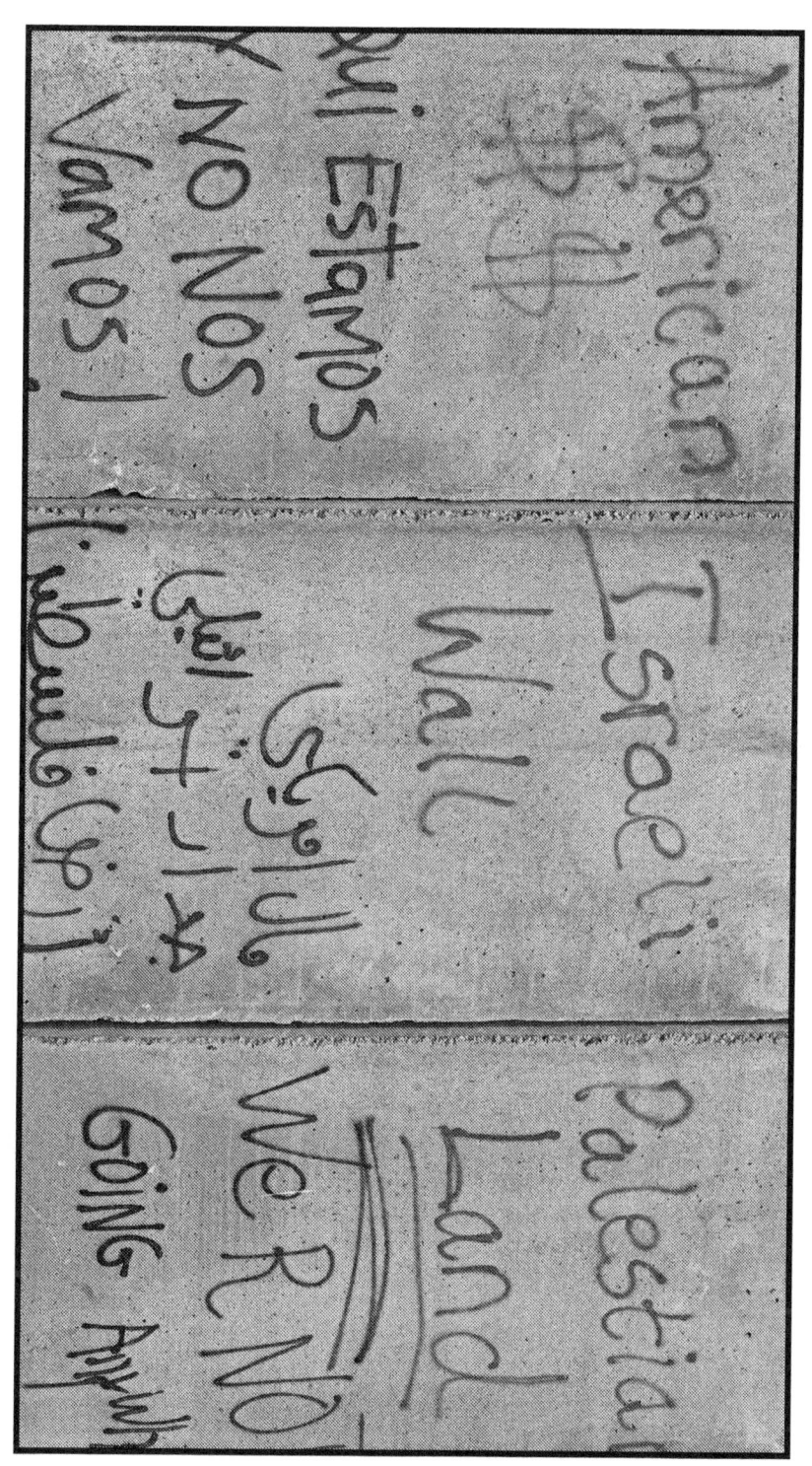

HILLARY IN GILO

HILLARY IN GILO

HILLARY IN GILO

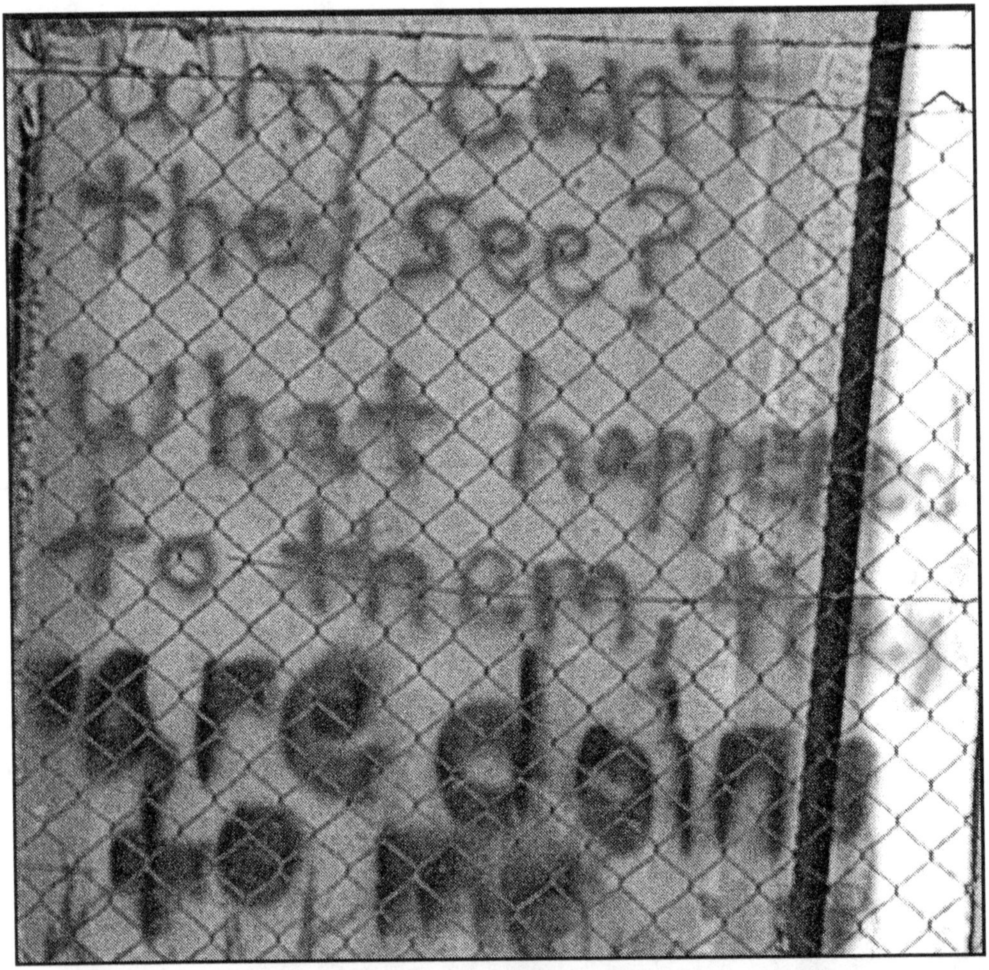

HILLARY IN GILO

CRUSADERS, ISRAELI FAKE "ARCHAEOLOGY" AND AN UGLY NEW JEWISH OUTPOST.

One day, on leaving Bethlehem and going to Jerusalem, I noticed for the first time that something was going on at the other end of Gilo, so I investigated.

I discovered a fascinating scene, but a truly depressing one. There must have been a number of Crusader-era buildings that had lined the road from Jerusalem to Bethlehem for a thousand years. Now I was witnessing their demolition. I can only imagine what had already been destroyed. I took photos of some of the remnants. But from the numerous mounds of rubble and stones piled up everywhere, on the sides of new roads and in the midst of fields, there must have until recently been many other buildings.

These Crusader buildings had carried a tremendous amount of history with them, good or bad. Physical reminders of our history, even painful history, should be preserved so we do not forget. These buildings had survivied a thousand years, whether from benign neglect or because people had converted them for their own use. The Palestinians had preserved many of the Crusader-era structures by converting them to their own use.

Now the Israelis, as they had done consistently from 1948 (though then more simply, with dynamite), were demolishing these historically priceless structures to erase the past of this land. And in their place -- another ugly Jewish trailer outpost.

If you were to ask an Israeli, I am sure that this destruction would be describd as some sort of careful and important "archaeological" work, the same fakery as with King David's City and the other digs around Jerusalem's Old City.

The Greek Monastery of Mar Elias in Beit Jala is just outside Bethlehem on the right side of Route 60 going to Jerusalem. On the left side is the portion of Beit Jala taken by the Israelis to build Gilo, and now they are also building there a new trailer park or outpost. The Monastery was founded in the 6th Century but rebuilt by the Crusaders in the 12th Century. The same type of building materials and style can be seen in the ruins scattered over the hills across from the Monastery, where the new Jewish outpost is being developed, and in the remaining Crusader buildings that are being destroyed by the Israelis.

The view in these two photos is from the Gilo side of Route 60 towards the Greek Monastery of Mar Elias in the background.

These, and the photos on the following pages, are the ruins, piles of rubble and the Crusader building remains on the Gilo side of Route 60.

HILLARY IN GILO

As the Crusader Period was short-lived (1099 - 1187, 1229 - 1244), these buildings, like the Mar Elias Monastery across Route 60, would be about a thousand years old. They could have survived that long only if the local populations had converted them to their own use, as the Palestinians seem to have done with these buildings (note what appears to be a metal beam and metal rebars in the photo below).

All of them are now being demolished by the Israelis to make way for the expansion of Gilo in the form, at least initially, of trailer homes.

HILLARY IN GILO

HILLARY IN GILO

The crosses to the right and in the enlarged photo on the next page are called the Latin or Roman Crosses. There appear to have been other symbols in the center (now just an empty circle) and at the top which were deliberately removed.

Over an arch of the same building (photo below), the middle cross is the Knights Templar Cross (also called St. John's or Maltese Cross). I cannot determine what the other circular crosses, on either side of the Templar Cross, represent. (Incredibly, traces of deep blue paint appear around the Templar Cross in my original color photos.)

These are photos of the new Jews-only trailer park or outpost going up in the same area as the disappearing Crusader buildings. The outpost, though it looks temporary, is starting the same way most of the settlements in the West Bank did.

First with a few "extremists" in trailers brought in during the night, ostensibly contrary to Government restrictions; then water, elecricity and sewage systems are supplied by some Government agency, on or off the books; then other municipal services, like bus service; and, from the beginning, protection by soldiers. Note the mounds of rubble and stones from destroyed buildings along the sides of the new roads being gouged out of the land for this new outpost.

SEWERS

BUSES

WATER AND DRAINAGE

ELECTRICITY

HILLARY IN GILO

THE AUTHOR IN THE WEST BANK

Born on August 8, 1939 in the Sunset Park area of Brooklyn. educated at Xavier High School in Manhattan (1957); Georgetown College (1961) and Cornell Law School (1964). Now lives in Manhattan, NY and Belmar, NJ.

(Photos courtesy of Barbara "Basha" Schanberg.)

www.ingramcontent.com/pod-product-compliance
Lightning Source LLC
Chambersburg PA
CBHW081456040426
42446CB00016B/3273